I0468258

Time Management

The Ultimate Guide On How To Stop Procrastination And Manage Your Time More Effectively

Before You Begin

>>Click Here For Your FREE Gift!<<

Introduction

This book contains proven steps and strategies on how to manage your time in the most effective way and how to stop distractions that prevent you from being productive.

One of the things that set successful people apart from the rest is their ability to manage their time effectively. Time is an important aspect in every person's life. You need to understand that you can no longer bring back hours that passed. This is why it is important that you know how to maximize your time that will allow you to finish all your tasks in the specified timeframe.

This book will shed light to the many benefits of effective time management. You will also learn some useful tips and techniques on how you can manage your time well and avoid distractions to be a successful individual. You will learn the important of making effective plans, optimizing your time, identifying and eliminating distractions, and some other tips that can lead you to a more productive life.

© Copyright 2016 All rights reserved.

This document is geared towards providing exact and reliable information in regards to the topic and issue covered. The publication is sold with the idea that the publisher is not required to render accounting, officially permitted, or otherwise, qualified services. If advice is necessary, legal or professional, a practiced individual in the profession should be ordered.

- From a Declaration of Principles which was accepted and approved equally by a Committee of the American Bar Association and a Committee of Publishers and Associations.

In no way is it legal to reproduce, duplicate, or transmit any part of this document in either electronic means or in printed format. Recording of this publication is strictly prohibited and any storage of this document is not allowed unless with written permission from the publisher. All rights reserved.

The information provided herein is stated to be truthful and consistent, in that any liability, in terms of inattention or otherwise, by any usage or abuse of any policies, processes, or directions contained within is the solitary and utter responsibility of the recipient reader. Under no circumstances will any legal responsibility or blame be held against the publisher for any reparation, damages, or monetary loss due to the information herein, either directly or indirectly.

Respective authors own all copyrights not held by the publisher.

The information herein is offered for informational purposes solely, and is universal as so. The presentation of the information is without contract or any type of guarantee assurance.

The trademarks that are used are without any consent, and the publication of the trademark is without permission or backing by the trademark owner. All trademarks and brands within this book are for clarifying purposes only and are the owned by the owners themselves, not affiliated with this document.

Chapter 1: What Are the Benefits of Effective Time Management?

It is true that the saying 'time is gold' is cliché, but you still need to take it seriously because time is a vital part of everyday life. It is even more important than money because you cannot bring back time and change the way you spent it. You need to know how some strategies on how you can manage your time more effectively. You should avoid making excuses about keeping your life organized, saying that you do not have the energy to organize your life when in fact, it is your disorganization that causes you a lot of stress and makes you feel tired.

You can get a lot of benefits if you know how to manage your time effectively. Here are some of them.

Less stress

Managing your time effectively means less stress because you do not have to worry too much about looming deadlines. If you know how to manage your time well, you will be able to finish your tasks and projects way before the deadline. You will not feel as stressed because you do not have to rush to meet the deadline. While your peers are trying to beat the deadline, you can just sit back and relax because you have already finished your task. Less stress also means a happier and healthier life. You are happier because you have fewer worries and you are healthier because your stress level is not high.

Increased productivity

Another benefit of better time management is increased productivity. Productivity is the amount of work accomplished within a span of time. The more work you are able to finish in a short period of time, the more productive you are. You can get more things done if you can finish your tasks early on. For example, if you need to do finish several tasks and you are able to finish some of them before the deadline, you can still work on the remaining tasks so that you can finish everything in a shorter period of time. Increased productivity is not only beneficial to you as an individual but also to your company.

Fewer mistakes

If you are not rushing to finish your task, you are more likely to produce a high quality output that does not require rework. Overlooked details, mistakes, and forgotten steps often lead to rework which means additional work that requires additional time and effort. You need to try your best to produce high quality output the first time you did the project. This can only be done if you are not cramming or not rushing to finish the project. For instance, if you have been assigned to design a website and you have not started anything yet and your deadline is almost near, you will end up submitting a design that has low quality just to have something to submit on the deadline. This can be avoided if you start doing the project right after you learned about it. Your subpar website design will surely require revisions, which means extra time and energy on your part.

Hassle-free life

Effective time management also makes your life a whole lot easier. Proper time management means fewer conflicts and problems because you do not have to miss appointments and deadlines. You can avoid creating problems by always being on time and preparing for your daily tasks. It also prevents issues with your family, friends, coworkers, and boss if you know how to juggle your work and personal life.

Improves your reputation

When your boss observes that you always produce high quality work within the deadline, he will not hesitate to give you a promotion or recommend you for one because he sees that you are reliable and dependable. Only people who show dependability are fit to become leaders in an organization like your company. Your boss will know that he can depend on you because you deliver what is expected of you at all times. It is nice to know that someone in a higher position like your boss believes in you.

More opportunities

You also need to know that more doors will be opened for you if you know how to manage your time effectively. If you are seen as someone who is always at the top of his game, you will always be considered first for different opportunities such as promotion, being sent abroad, leading a group project, and so on. If you are an early bird, you are likely to be able to finish all your tasks on time, and if you are well-prepared, you will have more options because you still have plenty of time on your hands.

More time on your hands

Knowing how to spend your time wisely means having more time on your hands to do the things that really matter to you. You can look at it on a daily basis. If you have a lot of house chores and errands, you can finish all of them in the morning so that you will have the rest of the day for relaxing and doing your hobbies. At the workplace, if you are able to finish your work early, you can request for a leave of absence for a couple of days or so to go on a vacation with your family. Your boss will be more than willing to say yes because he wants his top performing employee to relax and unwind so that he can be more productive when he returns.

These are some of the benefits of managing your time effectively. The next chapters will provide you with some helpful tips and tricks on how to manage your time effectively and stop distractions that lead to a more successful life.

Chapter 2: Optimize Your Time

One of the most important tips that you need to know to effectively manage your time is to learn how to optimize your time. Optimizing your time means getting the most out of your normal days. At the end of the day, you should be satisfied with the way you spent your waking hours because there is no time for regrets in life. Optimizing or maximizing your time is the first step to effective time management. Here are some useful tips for optimizing your time.

Start early

If you start your day early, you will also finish your tasks early. If you always wake up at 7am because you have to be at work at 8am, you should consider waking up at 6am instead. You can use the extra one hour every morning to finish house chores, do some exercises, and so on. If you start your day early, you will have plenty of time to relax when you return from work. It may be difficult at first especially if you are not a morning person but you will soon get used to it. Besides, waking up early in the morning while the rest of the world (or at least the rest of your household) is still sleeping gives you that much needed peace of mind that you need to get through the day. And the feeling of being productive at an early hour gives you the right kind of energy and motivation that will make you even more productive throughout the day.

Pay for services

Instead of spending your hard-earned money buying things that you do not really need, like another pair of shoes or another bag, you should consider spending your money on services that will make your life easier. The key is to spend money on things that free up time and not on things that take up space in your house. You can pay for a weekly cleaning service to free up a few hours every weekend, a lawn mowing service to clear the weeds in your front yard, or a laundry service so that you do not have to spend time washing your clothes. Besides, who needs a hundred pairs of shoes or hundreds of different outfits? Accumulating stuff will only make your life and home more cluttered, which means you need to spend more time cleaning up and searching for the object that you are looking for. And this is something that you want to avoid.

Use time optimization tools

Today's technology makes it easier for you to make the most out of your time. For example, your smart phone can make your life so much easier by combining several tools in one. You no longer need to buy an alarm clock, a planner, and an address book because you can find all these features in your smart phone. Some smart phones even allow you to create spread sheets that you can use for budgeting and other lists. You can also use your smart phone as a camera, video, GPS, music player, and so on. This means that you no longer need to waste your time remembering all the things that you need to bring when you go out.

Aside from using a smart phone, you can also invest in a wireless all-in-one printer that allows you to print files from multiple devices. It also has scanning features that you can use if you want to go paperless. In the kitchen, you can buy a crock pot which can basically cook your meals for you without having to check on it all the time and a food processor to make chopping and pureeing a lot easier.

Automation

Another way to optimize your time is to make use of automation in your life whenever you can. Automation is becoming more and more popular because it makes life so much easier. For example, instead of paying your bills manually one by one, you should consider enrolling in automatic payment where your payment will be automatically deducted from your bank account. Another way to automate your life is to automate your home. Many homes these days are fully automated. The thermostat, alarm system, security cameras, and other features in your house can now be controlled using one remote control. You can install smart lighting that allows you to set the timer so that it will turn on and off at your desired times. These smart home features make you feel more at ease even when you are on a long vacation because you know that your house is well-protected.

Streamline your tasks

This basically means simplifying your tasks to make them a lot easier. For example, instead of grocery shopping every day, you should consider doing it every week so that you do not need to go to the supermarket multiple times during the week. You can also avoid wasting your time thinking about what meal to prepare every day if you create a weekly meal plan. The meal plan will also let you know what items to buy when you go grocery shopping.

Chapter 3: Make Effective Plans Ahead of Time

Another way to manage your time effectively is to make plans ahead of time. If you plan your day ahead of time, you will find it easier to finish tasks on time. Planning your day means knowing what you are going to do at specific time frames. To give you some tips for effective planning that can lead to effective time management, you can check out the following paragraphs.

Create a schedule

You cannot manage your time effectively if you do not have a schedule for the day. Your schedule should include all the things that you need to do in a day and the allotted time for each task. Your schedule should starts from morning upon waking up until evening before going to bed. Some people who are extremely disciplined even include regular routines in their scheduler such as eating breakfast or taking a shower. You do not really need to add these in your schedule if you prefer to include only the important things, such as your workload, your children's school activities that you need to attend, dental appointments, and other tasks that change from time to time. By creating a schedule, you will know what you are supposed to be doing at a specific time. This will keep your tasks organized by letting you know what tasks you should finish first.

Create a meal plan

As what has been mentioned previously, creating a meal plan for the rest of the week also makes your life a lot easier. If you plan your daily meals for the whole week, you do not have to worry about what meal to prepare for breakfast, lunch, and dinner every day for 7 days. Creating a 7-day meal plan also makes grocery shopping a lot easier because you already know what you will need for the rest of the week. This limits your grocery shopping trips to one from several shopping trips in a week. Another benefit of creating a meal plan is that you can prepare healthy meals for your family. Eating takeout pizza and going out for dinner will be minimized because you already have your meals planned for the rest of the week.

Set goals

Aside from your daily schedule, you should also set goals, both short-term and long-term, to effectively manage your time. If you set goals, you can make sure that everything you do every day is geared towards achieving your goals. For example, if your goal is to get promoted, you have to make sure that you accomplish your workload on time. If your goal is to lose weight, you have to make sure that you allot at least an hour a day to exercise. If you know what you want to achieve, you will know how you should be spending your time.

Make lists

One very useful technique for planning ahead is making a list. Lists are essential if you do not want to forget anything, unless you have photographic memory that allows you to remember everything you need to do and at what time. You can make a to –do list with all the things that you need to do for the day, a grocery shopping list before your shopping trip, and other lists that can serve as your guide to effectively manage your time. Some people prefer to live their life with lists while others think that abiding by what is written on the list can be limiting. However, one thing that you should keep in mind is that making a list does not mean that you are not allowed to enjoy life and do things that you want to do. Lists only help you remember your tasks and monitor your progress so that you will have plenty of time later on doing your hobbies and interests.

Be realistic

When it comes to making plans, you have to be realistic or you are just setting yourself up for disappointment. Your allotted time for each task should be realistic. For example, if one project requires several days to finish realistically speaking, you should not force yourself to finish it in one day because that's what you have written down in your schedule. You have to maximize your time and finish tasks at the shortest time possible but make sure that your schedule is still realistic. Remember that you are not a robot. Your mind and body also need to recharge and working all day non-stop and setting an unrealistic deadline for yourself will only make you feel stressed out, which can in turn make you less productive.

Break large tasks into smaller tasks

Another tip for effective planning is to break large tasks into smaller tasks and set a deadline for each small task. For example, if your task is general cleaning, it will be more helpful for you if this is broken down into smaller tasks, such as cleaning one room at a time, finishing tasks in each room, and so on. If you just write down 'general cleaning' and you schedule it for one whole day, you will still have a hard time finishing this task because you do not know where to begin and how much time you should be spending on each room. It is not enough that you have the right skills for financial budgeting. It is also important that you know how to budget your time wisely.

Chapter 4: Prioritize Your Tasks

Prioritizing is a skill that you must have if you want to better manage your time. Many people complain that 24 hours a day is not enough to accomplish all the things that they need to do. This is not true. 24 hours is more than enough if they know how to prioritize their tasks. Prioritizing is simply the process of choosing the most important things that you need to finish right away over the less important things that does not require immediate attention. It helps you identify what tasks should be at the top of your to do list and what tasks you can do some other time.

To help you learn how to prioritize your daily tasks, you can review the paragraphs below.

Know the difference between 'urgent' and 'important'

Many people confuse these two words when it comes to describing their tasks. You need to understand that some urgent tasks are not really important in the long run (although they are important at that specific moment) such as watering the plants after a long vacation or picking up the laundry because you do not have clothes to wear tomorrow. These are urgent tasks that require your immediate attention but in the long run, they do not really matter at all. On the other hand, there are tasks that are important but are not urgent, such as improving your skills or spending more time with your family. Then there are tasks that are both urgent and important in the long run, such as finishing a project that is due today that can affect your promotion in the future. The trick here is to get rid of all the urgent and important tasks as soon as you can so that you can focus next on important tasks that are not too urgent.

Categorize your tasks based on the consequences

Another way to prioritize is to understand the consequences if the specific task is not done today. You can group all tasks that will result to serious consequences when not finished as soon as possible in category A. Some examples of tasks that you can include in this category is submitting your work due today or returning the phone call of an irate customer which is also scheduled today. Tasks under category B are those that can lead to slightly negative consequences if you do not finish them today. For example, not doing the large pile of laundry today means you do not have anything decent to wear when you go to work. There is a negative consequence but it is not as serious as the first category.

Category C tasks are those that have no penalty or negative consequences when not done today but should still be done, like changing your curtains or organizing your office cubicle. Then there are tasks that you can include in category D, or the category for tasks that you should delegate to other people. Category E tasks are activities that you can eliminate to shorten your to-do list, like going to the year-end sale to hunt for bargains or something not so important.

Arrange your list from most to least important

When making a list, the most important and urgent tasks should be at the top of your list so that they are the first thing that you will see when you look at your to-do list. Those that you have placed at the bottom of your list are tasks that can be done some other day, but it would still be nice if you can finish everything in your list within the day. By organizing your list, you will know which ones require your immediate attention and which ones do not. This will prevent you from feeling overwhelmed with all the things that you need to do.

Identify the times when you feel most energetic

The time when people usually feel most energetic is early in the morning. This should be allotted to doing category A or B tasks so that you can accomplish more in a shorter period of time. Category C tasks should not be schedule during your peak hours because it will just be a waste of energy. Of course, this depends on the person. Some people feel most energetic after lunch while others are more alert at night.

Some considerations

There are some considerations that you need to know when prioritizing your tasks. For example, if you need to attend a meeting early in the morning but the meeting is in your category B task, and then you have no choice but to put it at the top of your list. This means that prioritizing tasks also depends on existing factors that you have no control over. Another example is exercising. It may be a category C task but if you prefer doing it in the morning to give you a boost of energy, you should do it before you start your day. You should also consider the weather because some tasks are affected by the weather or the schedule of other people involved in completing the tasks.

Chapter 5: Eliminate Sources of Distractions

Distractions keep you from achieving maximum efficiency and productivity. Those people who always regret the way they spent their time every day usually give in to distractions. In today's modern world, there are so many sources of distractions like cell phones, internet, video games, and TV. If you want to manage your time effectively, you need to identify and eliminate your sources of distraction so that you can get more work done. Here are some tips and tricks that you need to know.

Check your email once or twice a day

Some people waste their time checking their email several times a day. Do not keep your email open while you are working because you will be tempted to check it every few seconds. Limit yourself to checking your email once or twice a day. You should schedule replying to important emails, like once in the morning and another in the evening. This way, you will not check your email multiple times a day because you know that there is an allotted schedule for this.

Turn off phone notifications

Smart phones are extremely useful when it comes to optimizing your time but they can also be a source of distractions. When your phone bleeps whenever there is a notification—whether it is a notification from your email, reminders, apps, or games—you are tempted to look and check what is the notification all about it. And before you know it, you are checking your email again, commenting on a friend's status update on Facebook, or cooking meals in your virtual restaurant. Some even go as far as turning off their smart phones completely when doing important work so that they won't be bothered by these notifications.

Disconnect from the internet

One effective way to avoid distractions is to disconnect from the internet if you do not need to go online while working. Closing Facebook and Twitter tabs is not enough for most people because they can easily open the page whenever they want. The best way it to disconnect your laptop from the internet while you are working. If you need to go online to do your research, you should do your research in one go then disconnect from the internet. This way, you can focus on your work and not on stalking your ex's Facebook account or reading internet memes.

Remove clutter

Clutter can also be a cause of distraction, whether it is physical or digital clutter. You should get rid of those items littering your office table because these can be a source of your distraction. Having a visual clutter will keep you from focusing on your work. This is also true with digital clutter. You should get rid of clutters in your life whether it is at home or at work to effectively manage your time.

Find a quiet place to work

Your probably have your own cubicle in your office that will keep you from distractions caused by your coworkers. If not, you can do something that will let your coworkers know that you are busy, such as wearing a headset or putting up a 'do not disturb' sign on your table.

If you are working at home, you should have your own office where you can work in peace. If you are working in your bedroom, you might be distracted by the warm and cozy bed that seems to call your name. If you are working in the living room, you may be distracted by your children's racket, the sound coming from the TV, and other distracting sounds in your house.

Establish a routine

If you establish a set of routine every day, you will not notice distractions as much because you are moving automatically. You do not have to think twice about doing a certain task if you have already established a routine. If you develop a routine that is free from distractions, you will be more productive because you can manage your time more effectively.

Chapter 6: Balance Work and Play

Effectively managing your time does not mean working nonstop without any time for breaks or vacation. This is not what this book is all about. This book aims to help you be more productive by finishing the tasks that you NEED to do so that you will have plenty of time to do the things that you WANT to do. It is important to keep the balance between work and play so that you further improve your productivity. If you refresh your mind and recharge your body, you will be more productive when you return to work. Here are some ways that you can balance work and play for better time management.

Take breaks

It is not a crime to take breaks even though you have a lot of important things to finish. Taking short breaks during work will help refresh your mind to keep you going. For example, after working in front of your computer for a couple of hours or so, you should consider taking a short break for a minute or two to stretch your legs and arms and to close your eyes. You should also avoid using your short breaks and lunch breaks to work no matter how much work you need to finish within the day. Most companies offer an hour for lunch break and two 15-minute breaks, one in the morning and another in the afternoon.

Take a vacation

To fully recharge, you should also take a vacation for a few days or weeks. Most companies allow their employees to go o paid vacation for 15 days or so. You can take one long vacation in a year to go abroad or several short vacations for simple family outings and get-togethers. This is also your chance to spend quality time with your family. When you take a vacation, you should avoid taking phone calls or taking work with you. A vacation is a vacation and it should be spend to relax and have a great time with your family.

Don't bring work at home

You need to work hard during office hours at the office but you should avoid taking your work at home. Your home is your sanctuary and the place where you can unwind and relax. If you bring unfinished work at home, you are also bringing unnecessary stress. Besides, you need to spend your time at work with your family. You spend most of your waking hours a the office and it is only right to spend the remaining hours when you are awake at home with your family.

Have a hobby

Being able to manage your time effectively leaves you with enough time to pursue your interests and hobbies. After working five days a week, it would be nice to do something that you want, like outdoor activities or playing sports. If you have a hobby, you have something to look forward to at the end of a long work week. You can also enroll in short courses like cooking or sewing during weekends or take up music lessons two or three times a week. Having a hobby makes your work and personal life more balanced.

Socialize

Socializing by hanging out with friends or attending parties should not make you feel guilty. It is important that you find time to socialize with your friends. It is important to spend time with your family but it is also important to spend time with friends. You can play games, go fishing, go to the beach, eat out, drink coffee, and do fun activities with your friends. You may be busy but do not cut your communication with these people who have been with you through thick and thin.

The key here is to keep the right balance between work and play which is the ultimate goal of effective time management.

Conclusion

The steps I have given you for successful time management will only be successful if you take action and implement the steps I have given you exactly as I have explained them. If you are only passively reading this book and not implementing these steps, you will not have success. Successful time management is about breaking habits of procrastination, which takes time.

I hope this book was able to help you to learn some useful tips and techniques on how to manage your time effectively and stop distractions.

The next step is to use the information in this book to your advantage that can help you effectively manage your time, stop distractions, and be more productive that can lead to your success.

www.ingramcontent.com/pod-product-compliance
Lightning Source LLC
Chambersburg PA
CBHW070428190526
45169CB00003B/1464